Newton's laws of motion
Unit Guide

The School Mathematics Project

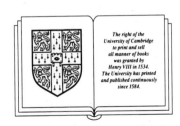

The right of the
University of Cambridge
to print and sell
all manner of books
was granted by
Henry VIII in 1534.
The University has printed
and published continuously
since 1584.

Cambridge University Press

Cambridge   New York   Port Chester   Melbourne   Sydney

Main authors	Stan Dolan
	Judith Galsworthy
	Andy Hall
	Mike Hall
	Janet Jagger
	Ann Kitchen
	Melissa Rodd
	Paul Roder
	Tom Roper
	Mike Savage
	Bernard Taylor
	Carole Tyler
	Nigel Webb
	Julian Williams
	Phil Wood
Team leader	Ann Kitchen
Project director	Stan Dolan

This unit has been produced in collaboration with the Mechanics in Action Project, based in the Universities of Leeds and Manchester.

The authors would like to give special thanks to Ann White for her help in producing the trial edition and in preparing this book for publication.

Published by the Press Syndicate of the University of Cambridge
The Pitt Building, Trumpington Street, Cambridge CB2 1RP
40 West 20th Street, New York NY 10011–4211, USA
10 Stamford Road, Oakleigh, Melbourne 3166, Australia

© Cambridge University Press 1991

First published 1991

Produced by Gecko Limited, Bicester, Oxon

Cover design by Iguana Creative Design

Printed in Great Britain at the University Press, Cambridge

British Library cataloguing in publication data

16–19 mathematics.
  Newton's laws of motion
  Unit guide
  1. Mechanics. Mathematics
  I. School Mathematics Project
  531.0151

ISBN 0 521 40878 4

Contents

Introduction to 16–19 Mathematics

Nobody reads introductions and nobody reads teachers' guides, so what chance does the introduction to this unit guide have? The least we can do is to keep it short! We hope that you will find the discussion point and tasksheet commentaries and ideas on presentation and enrichment useful.

The School Mathematics Project was founded in 1961 with the purpose of improving the teaching of mathematics in schools by the provision of new course materials. SMP authors are experienced teachers and each new venture is tested by schools in a draft version before publication. Work on *16–19 Mathematics* started in 1986 and the pilot of the course has been used by over 30 schools since 1987.

Since its inception the SMP has always offered an 'after sales service' for teachers using its materials. If you have any comments on *16–19 Mathematics*, or would like advice on its use, please write to:

> 16–19 Mathematics
> The SMP Office
> The University
> Southampton SO9 5NH

Why 16–19 Mathematics?

A major problem in mathematics education is how to enable ordinary people to comprehend in a few years concepts which geniuses have taken centuries to develop. In theory, our view of how to pass on this body of knowledge effectively and pleasurably has changed considerably; but no great revolution in practice has been seen in sixth-form classrooms generally. We hope that, in this course, the change in approach to mathematics teaching embodied in GCSE schemes will be carried forward. The principles applied in the course are appropriate to this aim.

- Students are actively involved in developing mathematical ideas.
- Premature abstraction and over-reliance on algorithms are avoided.
- Wherever possible, problems arise from, or at least relate to, everyday life.
- Appropriate use is made of modern technology such as graphic calculators and microcomputers.
- Misunderstandings are confronted and acted upon.

By applying these principles and presenting material in an attractive way, A level mathematics is made more accessible to students and more meaningful to them as individuals. The *16–19 Mathematics* course is flexible enough to provide for the whole range of students who obtain at least a grade C at GCSE.

Structure of the courses

The A and AS level courses have a core-plus-options structure. Details of the full range of possibilities, including A and AS level *Further Mathematics* courses, may be obtained from the Joint Matriculation Board, Manchester M15 6EU.

For the A level course *Mathematics (Pure with Applications)*, students must study eight core units and a further two optional units. The diagram below shows how the units are related to each other. Other optional units are being developed to give students an opportunity to study aspects of mathematics which are appropriate to their personal interests and enthusiasms.

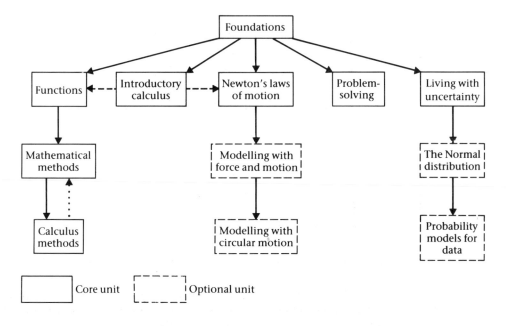

The *Foundations* unit should be started before or at the same time as any other core unit.

Any of the other units can be started at the same time as the *Foundations* unit. The second half of *Functions* requires prior coverage of *Introductory calculus*. *Newton's laws of motion* requires calculus notation which is covered in the initial chapters of *Introductory calculus*.

The chapter on polynomial approximations in *Mathematical methods* requires prior coverage of some sections of *Calculus methods*.

For the AS level *Mathematics (Pure with Applications)* course, students must study *Foundations*, *Introductory calculus* and *Functions*. Students must then study a further two applied units.

Material

In traditional mathematics texts the theory has been written in a didactic manner for passive reading, in the hope that it will be accepted and understood – or, more realistically, that the teacher will supply the necessary motivation and deal with problems of understanding. In marked contrast, *16–19 Mathematics* adopts a questing mode, demanding the active participation of students. The textbooks contain several devices to aid a more active style of learning.

- Topics are opened up through **group discussion points**, signalled in the text by the symbol

  and enclosed in rectangular frames. These consist of pertinent questions to be discussed by students, with guidance and help from the teacher. Commentaries for discussion points are included in this unit guide.

- The text is also punctuated by **thinking points**, having the shape

  and again containing questions. These should be dealt with by students without the aid of the teacher. In facing up to the challenge offered by the thinking points it is intended that students will achieve a deeper insight and understanding. A solution within the text confirms or modifies the student's response to each thinking point.

- At appropriate points in the text, students are referred to **tasksheets** which are placed at the end of the relevant chapter. A tasksheet usually consists of a self-contained piece of work which is used to investigate a concept prior to any formal exposition. In many cases, it takes up an idea raised in a discussion point, examining it in more detail and preparing the way for formal treatment. There are also **extension tasksheets** (labelled by an E), for higher attaining students, which investigate a topic in more depth and **supplementary tasksheets** (labelled by an S), which are intended to help students with a relatively weak background in a particular topic. Commentaries for all the tasksheets are included in this unit guide.

The aim of the **exercises** is to check full understanding of principles and give students confidence through reinforcement of their understanding.

Graphic calculators/microcomputers are used throughout the course. In particular, much use is made of graph plotters. The use of videos and equipment for practical work is also recommended.

As well as the textbooks and unit guides, there is a **Teacher's resource file**. This file contains:

- review sheets which may be used for homework or tests;

- datasheets;

- technology datasheets which give help with using particular calculators or pieces of software;

- a programme of worksheets for more able students which would, in particular, help prepare them for the STEP examination.

Introduction to the unit (for the teacher)

This unit is written as an introduction to Newtonian mechanics and mechanical modelling. Newton's laws of motion are therefore the end-point of the unit and not the beginning. The notation of the calculus is used but no further knowledge of advanced mathematics is required. In consequence, this unit has been found to be suitable for students who only have a GCSE mathematics background.

Parts of the unit will be easy for students who have a good grasp of GCSE physics. However, students should beware of being complacent because the unit requires a better conceptual understanding than a conventional approach to mechanics. Very able students should be able to move very quickly through the material of chapters 2 and 3 but should find plenty to challenge them in the investigative work throughout the unit.

The experiments should be tackled even if students have previously 'done' them in physics. The emphasis previously placed on the practical may not be appropriate here. In particular, students should be learning how to choose their own variables and how to interpret results that may differ from those expected using standard theory.

The unit lays great emphasis on the modelling process. The practical investigations are a vital part of learning the modelling process and should not be rushed. 'Setting up the model' enables students to define the problem for themselves without being spoon-fed with all the data and variables carefully laid out for them. Going from the real world to the mathematical world is not easy and students will need help and guidance. Equally, it is unwise to ignore the last stages of interpretation and validation. These are skills which must be taught if mechanics is to be anything other than a set of rules which have no relevance to the real world.

Some additional notes in the individual chapters may prove helpful.

Chapter 1

This unit starts with simple practical situations such as pushing the pedal on a bicycle. These give a feel for modelling in mechanics and it is vital that students should discuss and try them for themselves. In communicating their ideas, students may use words such as energy, velocity and acceleration. In many cases these words will be given their everyday meanings and not their mathematical meanings. One of the aims of the unit is gradually to teach the mathematical meaning of these words. For example, acceleration will not be dealt with until the final chapter which deals with Newton's laws of motion.

The experiments in tasksheet 1 should be referred to throughout the unit, either directly as in the case of 'Shoot', or indirectly by using the techniques learnt to study the practical further. This process ends in the last chapter when the students are asked to apply their knowledge of forces to their own experiment. This gives the students an opportunity to revise all they have met in a single context.

The modelling diagram is introduced as a description of, and a guide to, problem solving in applied mathematics. The context of Galileo's experiment is used to exemplify the stages. The modelling diagram is used repeatedly throughout the practical work and investigations in the unit, so it will be worthwhile spending a little time clarifying it here.

Chapter 2

The related concepts of distance, speed and time are developed in this chapter in a relatively straightforward way. The chapter therefore provides a good opportunity for stressing the simplifying assumptions which are necessary so that motion can be modelled mathematically.

It is important that students are encouraged to tackle the final tasksheet of the chapter at their own level. Extremely able students should attempt to develop sophisticated algebraic models for all investigative tasks.

Chapter 3

This chapter should also prove relatively straightforward for many students. It is important that the relationship concerning the displacement between two positions being the **change** in displacement from the origin should be thoroughly understood in the context of using vector triangles. This idea will be very useful in later chapters dealing with velocity and especially momentum.

Chapter 4

In this chapter, students should start to appreciate the importance of the distinction between scalar and vector quantities. Topics such as change in velocity and resultant velocity should be used to emphasise that there are considerable advantages in 'thinking vectorially'.

Students are likely to have found 'change in displacement' intuitively obvious. 'Change in velocity' also has a fairly straightforward relationship to students' experiences. This relationship can be strengthened by simple practicals, for example with clockwork cars on a mat. If the idea of a change in a vector quantity is understood at this stage, it will not cause any problems when tackled in a less 'obvious' context such as that of momentum.

Chapter 5

This chapter is the heart of the unit. Students are expected to start to wrestle with some of the misconceptions they may have about motion and how it is changed.

The simple experiments should help students to become aware that momentum is the fundamental 'quantity of motion' and that if there are no external influences this quantity will be unchanged or conserved. These experiments should, of course, be supplemented with others if necessary. For example, collisions of snooker balls are excellent for demonstrating the vectorial nature of the conservation of momentum law.

Chapter 6

This chapter rounds off the unit with Newton's laws of motion. The discussion point of section 6.2 is central to the chapter in that it provides some evidence that change of momentum per second measures the strength or force of a push or pull.

In the text, the laws of motion are applied to weight and the motion of objects moving freely under the Earth's gravitational attraction. Students will also find it valuable to return to the experiments of the first chapter and complete their report on the motion they observed.

Tasksheets and resources

1 Modelling motion

1.1 Mechanics today

Many simple everyday events have results we do not expect. For each of the situations below, decide what you would expect to observe. Check what happens in practice.

Think of other events involving motion which you have observed. Can your fellow students guess what happened?

The study of mechanics will help you to 'explain and predict' a range of events and phenomena in the physical world. This section will introduce you to the types of event in which we are interested, i.e. to which mechanics can contribute an important new insight.

You are **not** expected to provide the correct theoretical explanations at this stage. The point of this section is to direct your attention to the interesting questions you can ask about the world of mechanics and motion in which we live.

(a) If the small ball is on the top, it will rebound to a much greater height than it would if it were dropped on its own. The large ball hardly leaves the floor at all.

If the large ball is on top, the small ball stays near the ground, while the large ball bounces more or less normally.

(b) A full can takes the shorter time to roll down the slope. (However, a half-full can does not take a time halfway between those taken by the full and the empty cans.)

(c) The bicycle will roll backwards. Try the experiment yourself.

(d) (i) The reading stays the same.   (ii) The reading decreases.

Perpetual motion machines, the swirling of bathwater down a plughole and road banking angles are just a few of the many other interesting ideas you may have considered. Further examples are described in the following books:

Epstein, L.C., *Thinking Physics: Is Gedanken Physics?*, Insight, San Francisco, 1983.

Walker, J., *The Flying Circus of Physics*, J. Wein, New York, 1975.

1.2 Galileo's experiment

> Set up and conduct a similar experiment.
>
> What precautions should you take to make your results consistent?
> How can you ensure accuracy in the recording of your results?
> How can you set out your results clearly?
>
> What is the relationship between distance and time?

The aim of the experiment is to find the relationship between time taken and distance rolled as described in section 1.3. You should use this experience to help you to set up an experiment of your own in tasksheet 1. It is important at this stage to learn the art of good experimental practice! Some important points to remember are:

CONSISTENCY

It is important that each result is obtained by a set procedure, so that the experiment is repeatable. If a ball rolls 1 metre down the track in 2.2 seconds the first time, the experiment should be repeated to test how consistent this time is (within the degree of accuracy concerned). If the ball bounces from side to side, or if the measuring is done in a sloppy and inconsistent manner (e.g. from the front of the ball one time and the middle the next), then you should expect inconsistent results.

The following points may help.

(a) Practise timing before the experiment begins. Measure the time between two handclaps and compare your results with those of other students.

(b) Have as many stopwatches as possible.

(c) Call out '3, 2, 1, go' as you release the ball and let the ball hit a brick at the end of its measured run.

(d) Use a brick to hold the ball in place at the start. This will help you to get the correct distance between the start and the finish.

ACCURACY

What sources of inaccuracy are there? For example, in measuring time, there are delayed reactions. Can these cancel each other out at the beginning and end of the run?

The experiment should be set up to take at least 3 seconds for the ball to roll the full length of the track.

Discuss the use of the mean, mode or median in choosing which measurement to use in your analysis.

Galileo had difficulty measuring time accurately and records show that he had to design a special time-piece; he used a large flat vessel of water from which water was allowed to drip, the weight of the water released being measured to give the time.

REPEATABILITY

The data collected **must** be repeatable by other experimenters at other times. It is essential, therefore, that all pertinent details should be noted:

- type of track and ball;
- angle of slope;
- length of track;
- method of timing.

ANALYSIS

Having collected the data, a graph can be drawn and a function fitted to it. The points should be joined by some type of curve. A function graph plotter can be used.

The ball starts from rest and travels with increasing speed down the track. The results should give an approximation to $d = kt^2$. The shape of the graph is indicated below. As the slope of the track is increased, k increases. However, if the angle of the track is too great then it becomes impossible to measure t with accuracy. (Any result using a value of t smaller than 0.5 second is suspect.)

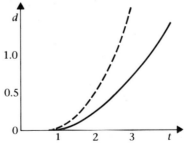

INTERPRETATION AND VALIDATION

The experiment should not stop here, but should be followed by:

- prediction of a given time for a roll of given distance, within the range of distances recorded (interpolation);
- validation of predictions by testing them practically.

Experiments

You may not understand any of the theory behind the experiments at this point. You must, however, learn how to record and interpret your results. The actual mechanics behind the answers will be explained at the appropriate point in the unit. You will then refer back to the results you obtained here and see how they fit into the theory.

It is important that data for the experiments are collected and kept for use later in the unit.

THE BRICKLAYER'S LAMENT

Some practical details:

- The pulley should be fixed securely in a vertical plane with the string moving freely without knots or snagging on the pulley.

- The system should be released from rest each time. This is easy to do if the string is held at the pulley and then released on the word 'Go'.

- Several runs will be needed to assess consistency and accuracy; obviously poor runs should be excluded.

Other practical problems may be encountered and you should learn how to solve them yourself.

The results should give a clear graph of time increasing with distance.

If the distances measured are great, the masses may reach a steady 'terminal' velocity due to the friction in the pulley.

If the distances are too small, then inaccuracies in timing may hide any clear relationship between distance and time. If friction is ignored, a relationship of the form $d = kt^2$ is expected.

Possible extensions include changing the masses, for example to 50 g and 60 g, and repeating the investigation.

You should make use of the modelling diagram in writing up your results.

SHOOT

Check for accuracy and consistency as before. Release from the same point each time, choosing a point from which the ball takes at least 3 seconds to roll 1 metre.

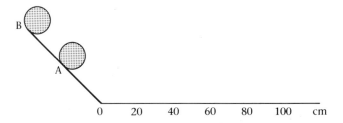

In the initial experiment the results depend on whether the times are measured from the release point A, or from when the ball reaches the start of the track at 0. These are shown by the thinner and thicker lines in the graph. The release point also affects the gradient of the graph.

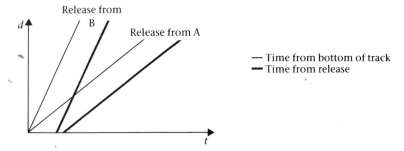

The second set of data collected for the ball rolling along the felt or ribbon will be used later to find the friction force involved. In this case, the (t, d) graph will not be linear as the ball will soon come to rest on the track.

PINBALL

The horizontal line at the base of the 'playing area' should pass through the base of the ramp as shown below. Release points 1 and 2 are too low to give a curve that fits most of the paper. Once again, to be consistent you must always release the ball from exactly the same height.

Care must be taken to avoid soaking the sugar paper with water or the ball will not roll properly.

The path traced out should be a parabola in all cases. The axis of symmetry may be found by folding the cut-out shape.

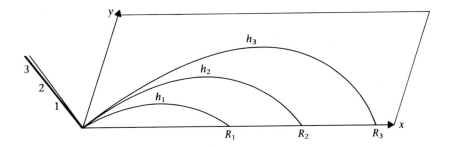

Discrepancies are caused by energy loss through friction or malformation of the ball. A snooker ball is probably best. The graph should have an equation of the form $y = kx(R - x)$, where R is the range.

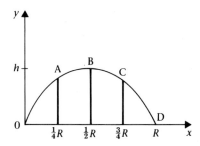

The release height is proportional to both h and R. It is also proportional to the square of the velocity at the bottom of the ramp.

If a ruler is laid across the path, then the times for the ball to travel through equal horizontal distances across the table can be found. This should show that the horizontal component of speed is constant.

2 Kinematics

2.2 Average speed

> Why is the overall average speed not simply $\dfrac{3+2}{2}$ =2.5 m s^{-1}?

Overall average speed does not mean the average of the different speeds. It means the constant speed at which the person must travel in order to travel the same total distance in the same time.

In the example given, the Scout travels 180 metres in the first 60 seconds and 360 metres in the first 150 seconds. His average speed for the first 60 seconds is therefore 3 m s^{-1} and his average speed for the first 150 seconds is $\frac{360}{150} = 2.4$ m s^{-1}

2.3 Graphs of distance against time

> What is represented by the gradient, $\dfrac{ds}{dt}$, of each of the
>
> lines above? What information do the corresponding $\left(t, \dfrac{ds}{dt} \right)$
>
> graphs convey about the athletes' motion?
>
> How realistic is this model? How could you improve your model of the motion of the runners?

The gradient, $\dfrac{ds}{dt}$, of a (t, s)

graph represents speed.

The corresponding $\left(t, \dfrac{ds}{dt} \right)$

graphs would show that the under-18 winner is faster.

(graph: vertical axis $\dfrac{ds}{dt}$ (m s^{-1}), horizontal axis t (seconds); horizontal line labelled "Under 18" above horizontal line labelled "Under 13")

The model is unrealistic because an athlete does not travel at a constant speed from the beginning to the end of a race.

More realistic graphs will be obtained from the 16–19 Mechanics video.

2.4 Distance and speed

> Describe some interesting features of the graph above.
>
> What does the graph tell you about the Scout's motion?
>
> How is the fact that the Scout walks and runs for equal distances represented in the graph?

There is a cycle which repeats itself every 150 seconds – the graph is **periodic** with period 150 seconds.

The graph consists of horizontal lines (which indicate that the speed is constant at either $2\,\mathrm{m\,s^{-1}}$ or $3\,\mathrm{m\,s^{-1}}$) with breaks at 60 seconds, 150 seconds, etc.

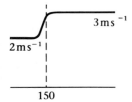

These breaks in a graph are called **discontinuities** and represent instantaneous changes in speed between $2\,\mathrm{m\,s^{-1}}$ and $3\,\mathrm{m\,s^{-1}}$. A more complicated graphical model of the motion might be as shown.

$$180\,\mathrm{m} = 3\,\mathrm{m\,s^{-1}} \times 60\,\mathrm{s} = 2\,\mathrm{m\,s^{-1}} \times 90\,\mathrm{s}$$

is represented by the **areas** underneath the $\left(t, \dfrac{ds}{dt}\right)$ graph, from time 0 to 60 seconds and from time 60 to 150 seconds respectively.

2.5 Speed

> When you say that a car is travelling at 30 miles per hour, does it mean that the car travels 30 miles every hour? If not, what does it mean and how can you measure speed as opposed to average speed?

The car would travel 30 miles in every hour only if its speed remained **constant** at 30 m.p.h. The speed of a car is said to be 30 miles per hour when, if the car continues to travel at that speed, it would travel 30 miles in each hour.

Rather than measuring the distance covered in an hour, you should measure the distance covered in a much smaller time interval. With very accurate measuring devices, an interval of one second would be more appropriate.

Scouts' pace

1 You will probably find that your measurements are quite different from those given in the text. When you are making your measurements, however, you must make sure that you model the same motion. Start running at a speed you can maintain for the 2 km of Scouts' pace, not your fastest sprinting speed. Do not just measure the length of one pace; try 20 paces and then divide by 20 to find the length of one pace. This will improve the accuracy of the measurement.

2 Your model will follow that in the text.

3 You may find that even though the assumptions made in the text were very crude, they gave a reasonably accurate estimate of the time taken to cover 2 km. However, this does not mean you have validated the model given in the text. The only way to validate your model is to go out and travel 2 km using Scouts' pace.

4 You may find that, for example:

    (a) running stride is always longer than walking stride;

    (b) running speed is always faster than walking speed;

    (c) the time for each stride is roughly constant, whether walking or running;

    (d) stride length depends on the length of leg of the walker, not on his or her overall height.

Scouts' pace

1 Analyse the problem.

The distance travelled in 40 paces running is 40 metres. The time taken for running is $\dfrac{40}{V}$ seconds.

The distance travelled in 40 paces walking is 40 metres. The time taken for walking is $\dfrac{40}{U}$ seconds.

The total time in seconds for 80 metres is $\dfrac{40}{V} + \dfrac{40}{U}$ or $\dfrac{40(U + V)}{UV}$.

The total time for 2 km is $\dfrac{1000(U + V)}{UV}$ seconds.

2 You will probably find that your measurements are quite different from those given in the text. However, when you are making your measurements, make sure that your model the same motion. Start running at a speed you could keep up for 2 km of Scouts' pace, not your fastest sprinting speed. Do not just measure the length of one pace; try 20 paces and then divide by 20 to find the length of one pace. This will improve the accuracy of the measurement.

3 It is most unlikely that the lengths of both your running stride and walking stride are equal to 1 m. You could therefore replace these by more realistic figures.

4 (a) Run and walk for equal lengths of time

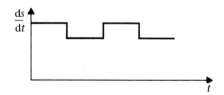

(b) Run, collapse and rest, run, etc.

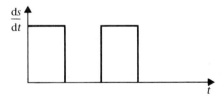

(c) Run, slow down, walk, run, etc.

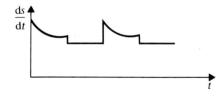

Walking to work

1 There will be many possible explanations of the shape of the graph. The intended journey is:

a walk up a hill;
a slow walk while waiting for a chance to cross a road;
a brisk walk to the main road;
a wait at a pedestrian crossing;
a walk to the office, slightly slowed down by the large number of students on their way to lectures.

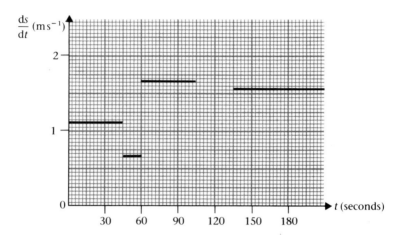

2 $\dfrac{ds}{dt}$ (ms^{-1})

3 On the (t, s) graph, the total distance of 250 metres is the height of the final point.

On the $\left(t, \dfrac{ds}{dt}\right)$ graph it is the sum of the areas under the horizontal line segments.

4 The fact that the lecturer was stationary is represented by a horizontal line on the (t, s) graph and by part of the t axis on the $\left(t, \dfrac{ds}{dt}\right)$ graph.

5 The lecturer travelled most quickly in the interval from 60 to 105 seconds. The (t, s) graph has its steepest gradient on this range. The $\left(t, \dfrac{ds}{dt}\right)$ graph is highest on this interval.

Galileo again

1 The ball's speed $\dfrac{ds}{dt}$ at that instant is 0.64 m s^{-1}. If its speed remained constant at 0.64 m s^{-1}, then its (t, s) graph would follow the dashed tangent from 2 seconds onwards.

2

Time in seconds	0.5	1	1.5	2	2.5	3
Gradient	0.16	0.32	0.48	0.64	0.80	0.96

3

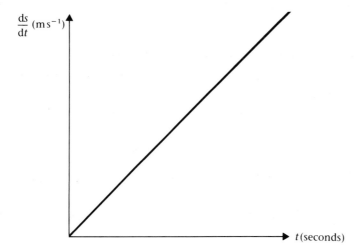

The $\left(t, \dfrac{ds}{dt}\right)$ graph is a straight line. The speed of the ball increases by approximately 0.32 m s^{-1} each second.

If you use your own data a curve should be drawn and the gradients found.

The $\left(t, \dfrac{ds}{dt}\right)$ points found using your gradients may not lie exactly on a line but you should have a set of points giving a good approximation to a straight line through the origin.

Overtaking

 Problem

To find the passing distance needed for a car to overtake a lorry moving at a steady speed.

MODEL 1

This is a simple model that makes a very good starting point.

Set up a model

Assume:
- the car has length 5 metres and is moving at a constant speed of $30\,\mathrm{m\,s^{-1}}$;
- the lorry has length 15 metres and is moving at $20\,\mathrm{m\,s^{-1}}$;
- they obey the two-second rule;
- the car takes t seconds to pass.

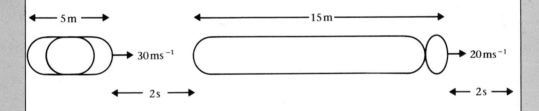

Analyse the problem

The car must travel $(5 + 60 + 15 + 40)$ metres if the lorry is stationary.

But the lorry will have travelled $20t$ metres so the total overtaking distance is $(120 + 20t)$ metres.

The car has speed $30\,\mathrm{m\,s^{-1}}$, so it will also have travelled $30t$ metres in t seconds.

Thus $\quad 30t = 20t + 120$
$$10t = 120$$
$$t = 12 \text{ seconds.}$$

Interpret /validate

The time taken to overtake safely is 12 seconds, during which time the car will have travelled 360 metres.

By choosing different values for the speed of the car you can see how the speed affects the distance needed to overtake.

Validation could be both difficult and dangerous!

MODEL 2

This is a model for those who like algebra.

Set up a model

Assume:
- the car has length 5 m and is moving at a constant speed of V m s^{-1};
- the lorry has length 15 m and is moving with constant speed U m s^{-1}
- they obey the two-second rule;
- the car take t seconds to overtake.

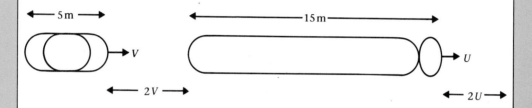

Analyse the problem

The car must travel $(5 + 2V + 15 + 2U)$ m if the lorry is stationary. But the lorry will have travelled Ut metres in that time, so the total overtaking distance in metres is $20 + 2(U + V) + Ut$.

But the car has travelled Vt metres, so

$$Vt = 20 + 2(U + V) + Ut$$
$$\Rightarrow \quad t(V - U) = 20 + 2(U + V)$$
$$\Rightarrow \quad t = \frac{20 + 2(U + V)}{V - U}$$

The distance travelled, s, is
$$s = Vt = \frac{2V(10 + U + V)}{(V - U)}$$

Interpret /validate

As $V - U$ increases, s decreases. The greater the difference in speed, the smaller the distance needed.

As V increases, the greater the distance needed to pass. This is because the car must pull out earlier if it is not to break the two second rule.

The greater the combined speeds of the two, the greater the distance. If $U > V$ then s is negative, i.e. passing is impossible. If $U = 0$ then the distance is $20 + 2V$.

3 Vectors

3.1 Introduction

A ship has sailed a distance of 10 km and drops anchor. What additional information do you need in order to locate its actual position?

With the information given, the ship could be at any point on the sea. Even if the starting point were known, its position could lie anywhere within a circle of radius 10 km, provided it was on the sea.

To fix its position completely you would need to know:
(a) whether the ship was sailing in a straight line or a curve or zigzag;
(b) the direction in which it was travelling;
(c) the point from which it started.

3.3 Adding vectors

There are two ways of giving a displacement – as a column vector or as a distance and bearing.

Do you really need two ways of describing the same thing?

Is one form of vector more useful than the other?

For practical purposes, such as the flight of an aeroplane or the movement of a ship, the sensible way of representing a displacement is by distance and bearing.

However, if displacements are to be combined, it is generally easier if column vectors are used.

Hence the usefulness of the form of vector depends on the purpose for which it is required.

Adding vectors

1 (a) $\overrightarrow{XZ} = \begin{bmatrix} 18.5 - 2.6 \\ 49.6 - 10.2 \end{bmatrix} = \begin{bmatrix} 15.9 \\ 39.4 \end{bmatrix}$

$\overrightarrow{XY} = \begin{bmatrix} 13.4 - 2.6 \\ 15.4 - 10.2 \end{bmatrix} = \begin{bmatrix} 10.8 \\ 5.2 \end{bmatrix}$

$\overrightarrow{YZ} = \begin{bmatrix} 18.5 - 13.4 \\ 49.6 - 15.4 \end{bmatrix} = \begin{bmatrix} 5.1 \\ 34.2 \end{bmatrix}$

(b) The sum of the eastwards components of $\overrightarrow{XY}$ and $\overrightarrow{YZ}$ is $10.8 + 5.1 = 15.9$, which equals the eastwards component of $\overrightarrow{XZ}$.

Also the sum of the northwards components of $\overrightarrow{XY}$ and $\overrightarrow{YZ}$ is $5.2 + 34.2 = 39.4$, which equals the northwards component of $\overrightarrow{XZ}$.

Therefore you can write $\overrightarrow{XZ} = \overrightarrow{XY} + \overrightarrow{YZ}$.

(c) (i) $XZ = \sqrt{(15.9^2 + 39.4^2)} \approx 42.5$

$\tan \alpha = \dfrac{15.9}{39.4} \Rightarrow \alpha \approx 22.0°$

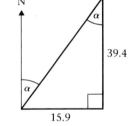

In going from X to Z the helicopter flies a distance of 42.5 km in the direction 022.0°.

(ii) $XY = \sqrt{(10.8^2 + 5.2^2)} \approx 12.0$

$\tan \beta = \dfrac{10.8}{5.2} \Rightarrow \beta \approx 64.3°$

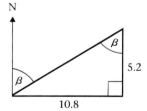

In going from X to Y it flies a distance of 12.0 km in the direction 064.3°.

(iii) $YZ = \sqrt{(5.1^2 + 34.2^2)} \approx 34.6$

$$\tan \gamma = \frac{5.1}{34.2} \Rightarrow \gamma \approx 8.5°$$

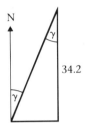

In going from Y to Z it flies a distance of 34.6 km in direction 008.5°.

2 $\overrightarrow{AB} = \begin{bmatrix} 4 \\ -2 \end{bmatrix}, \overrightarrow{BC} = \begin{bmatrix} 2 \\ 6 \end{bmatrix}, \overrightarrow{AC} = \begin{bmatrix} 6 \\ 4 \end{bmatrix}$

Notice that $\overrightarrow{AB} + \overrightarrow{BC} = \begin{bmatrix} 4 \\ -2 \end{bmatrix} + \begin{bmatrix} 2 \\ 6 \end{bmatrix} = \begin{bmatrix} 6 \\ 4 \end{bmatrix} = \overrightarrow{AC}$

3 $\overrightarrow{AD} = \overrightarrow{AB} + \overrightarrow{BC} + \overrightarrow{CD} = \begin{bmatrix} 2 \\ 2 \end{bmatrix} + \begin{bmatrix} 2 \\ 0 \end{bmatrix} + \begin{bmatrix} 3 \\ -4 \end{bmatrix} = \begin{bmatrix} 7 \\ -2 \end{bmatrix}$

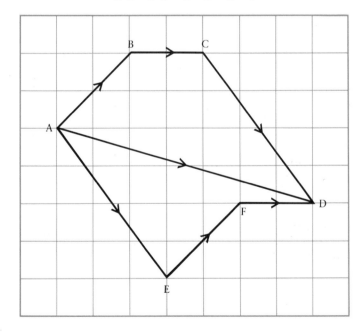

4 $\overrightarrow{AD} = \overrightarrow{AE} + \overrightarrow{EF} + \overrightarrow{FD} = \begin{bmatrix} 3 \\ -4 \end{bmatrix} + \begin{bmatrix} 2 \\ 2 \end{bmatrix} + \begin{bmatrix} 2 \\ 0 \end{bmatrix} = \begin{bmatrix} 7 \\ -2 \end{bmatrix}$

Notice that the resultant is the same, irrespective of the order in which the vectors are added.

4 Velocity

4.1 Speed or velocity?

> Points A to F show the car's position at 10-second intervals. Over what parts of the journey is
>
> (a)   the speed constant,   (b)   the velocity constant?

(a)   After slowing down to B, equal distances are covered in equal 10-second time intervals and so the speed is constant throughout the rest of the journey.

(b)   For the velocity to be constant, the direction of motion has to be in the same straight line **and** the speed must be constant, throughout the journey. The part of the journey for which this holds is from E to F.

4.2 Average speed and average velocity

> The village of Northaven is 30 kilometres due north of Southlea. One car travels from Southlea to Northaven at an average speed of 60 km h^{-1}. A second car does the same journey with an average velocity of 60 km h^{-1} due north.
>
> What precisely do the sentences above imply about the motion of these two cars? Do they in fact mean the same thing?

Average speed is obtained by dividing the distance travelled by the time taken to cover that distance. As the road winds from Southlea to Northaven, the distance **along the road** between them is more than 30 km and hence, travelling at 60 km h^{-1}, the car will take more than half an hour for the journey.

Average velocity is obtained by dividing the displacement between the start and finish of a journey by the time taken for the journey. The displacement between Southlea and Northaven is 30 km due north. Hence, if the average velocity of the second car is 60 km h^{-1} due north, the time taken for the journey is half an hour.

Equivalent constant speed and equivalent constant velocity can only have the same magnitude if the motion is wholly in a straight line in a given direction.

4.3 Straight line motion

Discuss this distinction for the cricket shown above.

If the batsman who has hit the ball takes two runs, he moves in opposite directions for each run. For the first run, the batsman will cover the distance between the 'popping creases'. (These are 1.22 m in front of each wicket, the distance between the wickets being 20.12 m.) Hence, in taking two runs, he will have covered a distance of $20.12 - 2 \times 1.22$ m = 17.68 m. (Technically, it will be the end of the bat that covers this distance – to save time, the batsman will ground the bat over the popping crease.) The distance he has covered at the completion of the second run is 2×17.68 m = 35.36 m. However, his displacement then is zero.

Mathematically, the direction of the first run can be taken as positive and the second run, in the opposite direction, as negative. It follows that the displacement of the first run is positive and that of the second is negative, but with magnitude equal to that of the first. Hence the total displacement will be zero. With the sign covention adopted, the displacement of the first run of the other batsman will be negative and that of the second run positive.

Velocity in the direction of the positive displacement will be positive and in the direction of the negative displacement it will be negative.

Speed has no sign.

If you are told the speed of the batsman is $8\,\text{m}\,\text{s}^{-1}$, you cannot tell whether he is on the first run or the second. However, a velocity of $8\,\text{m}\,\text{s}^{-1}$ means that he is on the first run and one of $-8\,\text{m}\,\text{s}^{-1}$ means that he is on the second run.

4.4 Change in velocity

> Find the new velocities of the cars.
>
> What is the change in velocity of each car?
>
> What relationship is there between the initial velocity of each car and its final velocity?

Car A The car moves 30 cm every second, relative to the mat, while the mat is simultaneously moving 40 cm every second in the same direction. Hence the velocity of car A is $(40 + 30)\,\text{cm s}^{-1} = 70\,\text{cm s}^{-1}$ in the direction of the motion of the mat.

Car B The car moves 30 cm every second, relative to the mat, in a direction opposite to that of the motion of the mat. The mat is simultaneously moving 40 cm every second.

Hence the velocity of car B is $(40 - 30)\,\text{cm s}^{-1} = 10\,\text{cm s}^{-1}$ in the direction of the motion of the mat.

Car C Every second the car moves 30 cm relative to the mat, perpendicular to the direction of the motion of the mat. The mat is simultaneously moving 40 cm every second.

The magnitude of the velocity of car C is 50 cm s^{-1}

$$\tan \theta = \frac{30}{40} \Rightarrow \theta \approx 36.9°$$

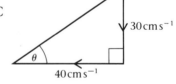

That is, the velocity of car C is 50 cm s^{-1} making an angle of 36.9° with the direction of the motion of the mat.

The change in velocity for each car is 40 cm s^{-1} in the direction of motion of the mat. In each case,

Original velocity + Change in velocity = New velocity.

For example, for car A

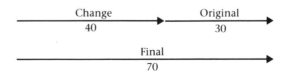

Shoot again

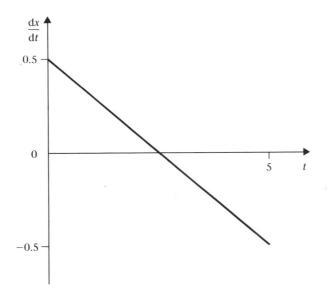

1   The graphs show that the furthest distance the ball travels from the bottom of the ramp is 62 cm. The ball is momentarily at rest when $t = 2.5$ seconds. The maximum speed of $0.5\,\mathrm{m\,s^{-1}}$ occurs when $t = 0$ and $t = 5$. The velocity changes from $0.5\,\mathrm{m\,s^{-1}}$ to $-0.5\,\mathrm{m\,s^{-1}}$.

2   The area under the $\left(t, \dfrac{\mathrm{d}x}{\mathrm{d}t}\right)$ graph represents the displacement.

3   If the area is underneath the t axis, then the ball is rolling down the ramp.

4   The velocity is   (a) $0.3\,\mathrm{m\,s^{-1}}$ (b) $-0.3\,\mathrm{m\,s^{-1}}$

5   The average velocity of the ball is   (a) $0.6 - 0.4 = 0.2\,\mathrm{m\,s^{-1}}$ (b) $0\,\mathrm{m\,s^{-1}}$

Point of no return

Problem

You are the pilot of a light aircraft which is capable of cruising at a steady speed in still air. You have enough fuel on board to last for four hours. What is the maximum distance you can safely fly from your base and still have enough fuel to get home?

Set up a model

The various factors to consider are:
(a) the velocity of the plane;
(b) the wind velocity;
(c) the altitude.

Assume that the velocity of the plane is constant and ignore the acceleration and retardation of starting and stopping. A speed of $150\,\mathrm{m\,s^{-1}}$ is reasonable for a light aircraft.

You may find it helpful to assume that the wind velocity is zero, in a preliminary calculation. Ignore the variation of fuel consumption with altitude. It is probably not significant for a light aircraft which will not fly very high.

Set up a model

M O D E L 1

Let the wind velocity be zero and the plane have velocity $150\,\mathrm{m\,s^{-1}}$.

Analyse the problem

Travelling at $150\,\mathrm{m\,s^{-1}}$ north for 2 hours gives a maximum distance from the base of $(150 \times 3600 \times 2)\,\mathrm{m} = 1080\,\mathrm{km}$.

Set up a model

M O D E L 2

Now let the velocity of the wind be $30\,\mathrm{m\,s^{-1}}$ south. Suppose that d metres is the maximum possible distance from base.

Analyse the problem

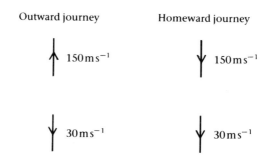

Outward journey   Homeward journey

$150\,\mathrm{m\,s^{-1}}$ $150\,\mathrm{m\,s^{-1}}$

$30\,\mathrm{m\,s^{-1}}$ $30\,\mathrm{m\,s^{-1}}$

On the outward journey the resultant speed is $120\,\mathrm{m\,s^{-1}}$ and the time taken is $d \div 120$ seconds.

On the homeward journey the resultant speed is $180\,\mathrm{m\,s^{-1}}$ and the time taken is $d \div 180$ seconds.

The total time must be 4 hours, so

$$\frac{d}{120} + \frac{d}{180} = 14\,400$$

$$\Rightarrow d = 1\,036\,800\,\text{(metres)}.$$

Interpret /validate

The maximum distance that you can fly from base and return safely is $1036\,\mathrm{km}$.

Set up a model

$MODEL\ \ 3$

Now generalise a little by letting the wind speed be $v\,\mathrm{m\,s^{-1}}$ south.

Analyse the problem

The resultant speed out is $(150 - v)\,\mathrm{m\,s^{-1}}$.
The resultant speed back is $(150 + v)\,\mathrm{m\,s^{-1}}$.

$$\frac{d}{150 - v} + \frac{d}{150 + v} = 14\,400$$

$$\Rightarrow d = 48\,(150^2 - v^2)$$

Drawing a graph of v
against d gives

Interpret /validate

When $v = 0$, then $d = 1080$ as in model 1.

The value of d is not altered if v is replaced by $-v$. Thus the result is the same whether the wind blows south or north. (Sketch the appropriate graph.)

If the velocity is greater than $150\,\mathrm{m\,s^{-1}}$ then d is negative and the aeroplane can never return to base!

As v increases then d decreases, slowly at first and then more rapidly.

5 Changes in motion

5.1 The 'quantity of motion'

> What makes a moving object easy or difficult to bring to rest?
>
> Consider different situations in which things at rest are set in motion. What makes it easy or difficult to move them?

First thoughts, together with everyday experience and observation, tell you that the faster something is travelling, the harder it is to stop. Conversely, the faster you wish something to go, the harder it is to achieve that speed.

You should also be aware that some measure of the quantity of the object is relevant. Clearly, it is not just the volume (compare the shot-putter's shot and the beach ball) and not just the concentration of matter, or density of the object – but a combination of the two. This combination, which is called the mass of the object, is not an easy idea and is explained in this section.

5.2 Collisions

> A Mini runs into the back of a large lorry which has stopped at traffic lights. What would you expect the motions of the Mini and the lorry to be like just after the collision?
>
> What would you expect if it had been the lorry running into the back of the Mini?

If the Mini runs into the lorry, the lorry will be knocked forward slightly, but not much. If the Mini does not become entangled in the back of the lorry, it may even bounce backwards a little.

If the lorry runs into the Mini, the Mini will be catapulted forwards rapidly. The lorry will be slowed down by the collision, but probably not stopped.

5.5 Change in momentum

> Find the change in momentum for each puck. What do you notice?
>
> Can you explain why this should happen?

For the puck of mass 0.1 kg, the momentum changes from 0.2 kg m s^{-1} towards the right to 0.1 kg m s^{-1} towards the left: a total change of momentum towards the left, of

$$0.1 - (-0.2) = 0.3 \, \text{kg m s}^{-1}$$

For the puck of mass 0.3 kg, the momentum change is from zero to 0.3 kg m s^{-1} towards the right.

So the momentum changes for the two pucks are equal in size and opposite in direction. You can conclude that the 'hit' experienced by one is equal and opposite to the 'hit' experienced by the other. The two changes in momentum cancel each other out if you look at the total momentum of both pucks. This is the law of conservation of momentum.

The quantity of motion

EXPERIMENT 1

The faster the snooker ball is rolled, the harder it is to stop and the more effect it has on the block which it hits.

This also occurs with the table tennis ball.

However, at any given speed, the table tennis ball is much easier to stop than the snooker ball and has much less effect on the brick.

EXPERIMENT 2

You should be able to feel a definite difference in the effort needed to stop the balls as they fall further. The further they fall, the greater their velocity.

> Is what you feel what Newton called the fundamental 'quantity of motion'?
>
> What do you think are the important factors which make up this quantity?
>
> Which do you think has more 'quantity of motion', a 4 tonne lorry travelling at $1\,\mathrm{m\,s^{-1}}$ or an 800 kg car travelling at $5\,\mathrm{m\,s^{-1}}$?

As a result of the experiments, the important factors of the quantity of motion are seen to be the mass and the velocity of the moving object.

A reasonable way of combining these would be by multiplying the two together, since the quantity of motion appears to increase with both mass and velocity.

If this is done for the lorry, the quantity of motion would be $4000 \times 1\,\mathrm{kg\,m\,s^{-1}}$. For the car the quantity of motion is $800 \times 5 = 4000\,\mathrm{kg\,m\,s^{-1}}$.

Thus the car and the lorry would have the same quantity of motion.

Collisions

GENERAL

When performing these experiments, you should not push the trucks so fast that a derailment occurs, nor should they be pushed so slowly that frictional effects would distort the results.

A rough idea of speeds can be gained without any detailed measurement or timing, although a ruler and watch can be used to improve accuracy a little. There is no need for more sophisticated timing methods in this experiment.

Initially, random selections of masses can be made. After a few attempts, the outcome of an experiment should be predicted **before** the experiment is performed. Conclusions can then be confirmed with a systematic choice of masses.

Results can be recorded easily in a simple table of possibilities and outcomes.

EXPERIMENT 1

When the two trucks are of equal mass, the moving one will stop and the initially stationary truck will move away. The speed with which the trucks separate can be seen to be roughly equal to the speed of approach.

When the moving truck is more massive than the stationary one, the moving truck will have its speed reduced and the initially stationary truck will move away with a greater speed than the initial speed of approach. The speed with which the trucks separate is again equal to the speed of approach, although this result may not be as apparent as in the case when the masses are equal.

When the moving truck is less massive than the stationary one, the trucks will move off in opposite directions after the collision. The direction of motion of the initially moving truck will therefore be reversed. The speed of separation is again roughly equal to the speed of approach.

EXPERIMENT 2

When the trucks have equal mass, it can be observed that the resultant speed of the joined trucks is roughly half of the moving truck's original speed. In general, if the two trucks have masses a and b then the resultant speed of the joined trucks is $\dfrac{a}{a+b}$ of the original speed of the moving truck of mass a, although this will be difficult to observe.

EXPERIMENT 3

There are many possible situations that can be studied. The following is a selection of possibilities with various masses and initial velocities.

(a) Both trucks moving towards each other so that they will stick together.
(b) Both trucks moving towards each other so that they will bounce apart.
(c) One truck chasing the other so that they will stick together.
(d) One truck chasing the other so that they will bounce apart.

In many cases, the conclusions will not be very clear. It is important to look out for situations which **do** give rise to clear results. For example, in case (b), a dramatic result occurs when the trucks have masses in the ratio $3:1$ and are moved together with the same speed. The more massive truck is brought to rest by the collision and the lighter truck has its direction of motion reversed and its speed doubled.

This is an excellent example of what is called an 'elastic' collision. The speed of separation ($2v$) is equal to the speed of approach ($v + v$).

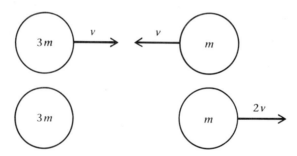

As with all the truck experiments, the total momentum is conserved. Momentum is a vector in the direction of motion with length equal to mass × speed.

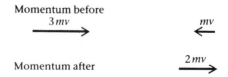

28

The effect of blows

EXPERIMENT 1

Once the ball is in motion on a horizontal surface it will be moving in a straight line with constant speed. On applying the blow at 90° to this straight line, the ball will be deflected at an angle to the original direction of motion and will continue to move in a straight line in the new direction, with a new speed.

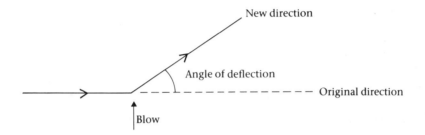

Varying the strength of the blow will vary the angle of deflection, the angle increasing as the strength of the blow increases.

The aspects of the motion being changed are the speed and direction, i.e. the velocity.

EXPERIMENT 2

If the blow is kept as constant as possible, it should be observed that the heavier balls are deflected less than the lighter ones.

EXPERIMENT 3

The paths of the two balls are shown below.

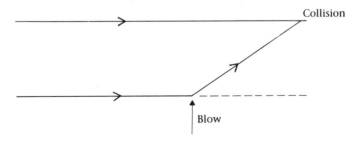

The ball which receives the blow should keep level with the other ball in the original direction of motion.

This shows that the blow, when applied at right angles to the original motion, does not affect the original motion along the horizontal surface. The blow gives the ball a component of velocity at right angles to its original direction while leaving the original component unchanged.

To summarise:
- if the mass is fixed, the change in velocity caused by the blow increases as the blow increases;
- if the blow is fixed, the change in velocity decreases as the mass increases;
- the blow changes the velocity in the direction of the blow.

Thus the blow changes the momentum in the direction of the blow. The change in momentum increases as the blow increases.

EXPERIMENT 4

One suggestion is to find what happens to the ball when the blow is delivered while it is still on the slope.

6 Force

6.1 Newton's first law of motion

> (a) Once a shot has left a shotputter's hand it does not travel in a straight line with constant speed. Why not?
>
> (b) Suppose your car has run out of petrol and you are pushing it along a level road. If you stop pushing it, it will soon stop moving. Why?

(a) If Newton's first law is to hold then there must be a force acting on the shot. That force is the pull of the earth on the shot, i.e. its weight. This gradually changes the velocity of the shot.

(b) There must be a force acting on the car to bring it to rest. This force is friction. (It might not come to rest if it is on a slope because then the weight of the car might overcome any frictional force.)

6.2 Newton's second law of motion

> (a) Use data from the practical 'Shoot' to find the change of momentum each second when the ball rolls along a strip of felt.
>
> (b) What do you think causes the momentum to change?

(a) The following results were taken from an experiment where the ball rolled along a strip of felt.

| Distance travelled (cm) | 0 | 60 | 80 | 100 | 120 |
| Time taken (seconds) | 0 | 0.7 | 1.0 | 1.4 | 2.0 |

These results can be compared with your own. However, the results will vary widely depending on the type of felt and the original speed of the ball.

Your results can be used to plot a (time, displacement) graph which will have the following shape:

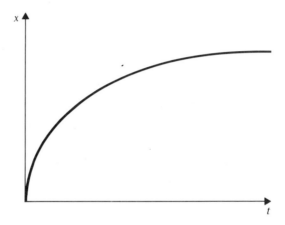

From this graph you can estimate the speed of the ball at various times. For the results above, the following can be obtained:

| Speed (cm s^{-1}) | 99 | 72 | 61 | 46 | 23 |
| Time (s) | 0 | 0.7 | 1.0 | 1.4 | 2.0 |

In this case the speed is dropping at a roughly constant rate of approximately 38 cm s^{-1} each second.

You should find that your data also yields a constant rate of change of speed. The rate of change of momentum for your ball will therefore also be constant.

(b) Newton recognised that rate of change of momentum was a measure of the resultant force being applied. In this case it indicates that there is a roughly constant frictional force acting on the ball.

6.3 Newton's third law of motion

Two students stand on skateboards and press against each others' hands. What can you say about:

(a) the force each exerts,

(b) their subsequent motion?

If one student is twice as heavy as the other, how does this affect your answers to (a) and (b)?

The skateboard experiment may be carried out practically. Subject to effects such as differences in the two skateboards themselves, you could expect

(a) the interaction forces of the two students to be equal in magnitude and opposite in direction;

(b) their momenta to be equal in magnitude and opposite in direction, at least initially.

The two students still exert the same force on each other, even if one is twice the weight of the other. Because their momenta are the same in magnitude, the heavier student will move off with half the speed of the lighter. (Note that if two skateboarders have a rope, they can pull towards one another in the same manner.)

6.4 Weight and change of momentum

(a) If a golf ball is allowed to fall freely, does the pull of the Earth change as it falls? Sketch the form of (time, velocity) graph you would expect.

(b) If a golf ball and cricket ball are dropped together, which will fall faster? Explain your answer.

(a) A set of scales registers the same weight for the golf ball no matter at what height they are used. The pull on the golf ball is therefore the same throughout its motion and so its momentum changes at a constant rate. The (time, velocity) graph will therefore be linear:

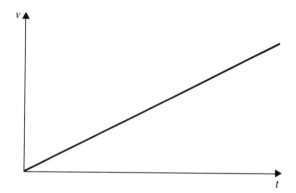

(b) Contrary to what many people believe, the rate at which an object falls does not depend upon its mass.

(You may have seen a film of the experiment performed on the Moon where, in the absence of air resistance, a feather falls at the same rate as a stone.) Air resistance has a negligible effect on the golf and cricket balls and so they have the same speed at any time.

Since the balls have the same speed at any time, their changes in momenta are in proportion to their masses. By Newton's second law, the resultant forces acting on them must be in proportion to their masses. The weight of an object is therefore a fixed multiple of its mass. This will be examined in more detail on tasksheet 1.

The 1 kg shot and the golf ball

1 (a) The velocity can be found by estimating the gradient of the (time, displacement) graph. Your estimates should be close to those shown in the table below.

Time t (seconds)	0	0.5	1.0	1.5	2.0
Velocity v (m s^{-1})	0	-5	-10	-15	-20

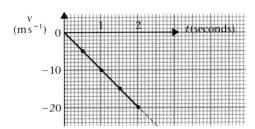

The (time, velocity) graph is shown above. The linear relationship shows that the magnitude of the velocity (the speed) is increasing at a steady $10\,\text{m s}^{-1}$. The velocity is negative because the direction is downwards.

(b) During the first second the momentum of the shot changes from 0 to $-10\,\text{kg m s}^{-1}$, and during the next second the momentum changes from -10 to $-20\,\text{kg m s}^{-1}$. The change in momentum is therefore $-10\,\text{kg m s}^{-1}$ during each second.

(c) You should expect the change in momentum to continue to be $-10\,\text{kg m s}^{-1}$ per second.

(d) According to Newton's second law, the change in momentum each second is a measure of the resultant force acting on the shot, so it would seem that there is a constant force of -10 newtons pulling the shot down. (The force is negative simply because it is acting in what has been taken to be the negative direction.) This is clearly the force of gravitational attraction.

It is interesting to note that if a second shot with a mass of $0.5\,\text{kg}$ had been released simultaneously with the $1\,\text{kg}$ shot, it would have had the same velocity and so its change in momentum would only have been $-5\,\text{kg m s}^{-1}$ per second. The force of gravitational attraction on a $0.5\,\text{kg}$ mass would therefore be $-5\,\text{N}$. The force of gravitational attraction would appear to be a constant $-10\,\text{N}$ per kg.

2 (a) The velocity can be expressed as a column vector.

Time	Velocity	
		$t=1$
1	$\begin{bmatrix} 10 \\ 20 \end{bmatrix}$	
		$t=2$
2	$\begin{bmatrix} 10 \\ 10 \end{bmatrix}$	
3	$\begin{bmatrix} 10 \\ 0 \end{bmatrix}$	$t=3$
4	$\begin{bmatrix} 10 \\ -10 \end{bmatrix}$	$t=4$
5	$\begin{bmatrix} 10 \\ -20 \end{bmatrix}$	$t=5$

(c) The tip of each momentum vector lies on the same vertical line. Therefore the horizontal component of momentum is the same in each case, and so the speed of the ball along the horizontal direction remains constant.

The change in momentum in each second is in the vertical direction.

Change in momentum during the 2nd second is $1\,\mathrm{kg\,m\,s^{-1}}$
Change in momentum during the 3rd second is $1\,\mathrm{kg\,m\,s^{-1}}$
Change in momentum during the 4th second is $1\,\mathrm{kg\,m\,s^{-1}}$
Change in momentum during the 5th second is $1\,\mathrm{kg\,m\,s^{-1}}$

(d) The change in momentum during each second is the same; $1\,\mathrm{kg\,m\,s^{-1}}$ downwards. The same constant rate of change of momentum is seen when a ball (or an apple) falls vertically downwards. It is caused by its weight, i.e the force due to the gravitational attraction of the Earth.